This belongs to:

_____

Ibn Abbas reported: The Messenger of Allah, peace and blessings be upon him, said to a man and he was admonishing him,

"Take advantage of 5 before 5:

your youth before your old age,

your health before your illness,

your riches before your poverty,

your leisure before your work,

and your life before your death."

اغْتَنِمْ خَمْسًا قَبْلَ خَمْسٍ:

شَبَابَكَ قَبْلَ هَرَمِكَ

وَصِحَّتَكَ قَبْلَ سَقَمِكَ

وَغِنَاكَ قَبْلَ فَقْرِكَ

وَفَرَاغَكَ قَبْلَ شُغْلِكَ

وَحَيَاتَكَ قَبْلَ مَوْتِكَ

[Mustadrak of Al-Hakim, Musnad Imam Ahmad]
Source: Shu'b Al-Iman 9575
Grade: Sahih (authentic) according to Al-Albani

Table of Contents

Table of Contents

Introduction

Productivity is defined as: **"A measure of the efficiency of a person in converting inputs into useful output/(s)."**

In short, productivity is about utilising whatever resources and abilities you have, in the most effective way possible.

Productivity is not about giving your all! It's about giving your BEST!

It's not only about development, it's about self-discovery.
It's not only about change, it's about awareness of yourself so you're able to fulfil the purpose of your existence in the best of manners in shaa Allaah.

This journal is a continuation of a gratitude journal that we launched in 2015 to help Muslim adults and kids find joy in the simplest of things with the power of **ALHAMDULILLAH.**

As students of Islamic psychology and Arabic language (after studying Qur'an extensively), this journal is a result of our studies and experiences.
And most of all, a result of our longing...We hope that your longing is fulfilled through this journal as well. And we really hope that you emerge as a more productive and better Muslim after using it in shaa Allaah.

Please remember us - AYEsha & samINA (AYEINA)
in your prayers if you benefit from it.
May Allah put immense Barakah in this journey for you
and make it a sadaqah jaariyah! Aameen.

How to Use This Journal

1) There is no right or wrong way to use it as there's no specific way to express yourself.
You do YOU!

2) Each category (<u>spiritual development</u>, <u>personal development</u>, <u>strengthening relationships</u>, <u>goals & dreams</u>) contains 7 watercolor illustrations along with several exercises to help you achieve your said goal with full conviction! These exercises often take a form of a chart, list or prompts & they don't need to be completed in any order.

3) There's space for your short term and long term goals at the end of each category. Fill them up with whatever you think has not been covered in the exercises & then track your progress in the given notes section. When you're done with one whole category, rate yourself in terms of productivity. Were you able to make the best use of it all?

4) You can take out the pages and stick them around your home to motivate yourself to keep going until you cross the finish line. [...**the reminder benefits the believers (51:55)**]

5) Adapt and make the exercises relevant for YOU! Write, erase, write again! Cry, laugh, get angry, start again! Skip pages or do them more than once! Shift them to the front so you can use the whiteboard with the whiteboard marker beside it. Customise it as you wish.

6) Fill it in a month or a year - whenever you're ready for some soul-searching...Add sticky notes or entire pages. Do it alone or with someone special. Assign them to fill a few pages for you if you feel stuck. Or help them find their own voice through it (you can even help children in the process of self discovery & development as long as they can write).

7) You can email us for a free printable template if you'd like to repeat some exercises. Subscribe to ayeina.com for extended printables if you want to further explore this journey.

It's time to peel back the layers and connect to your heart, body, mind and soul.
In Shaa Allaah

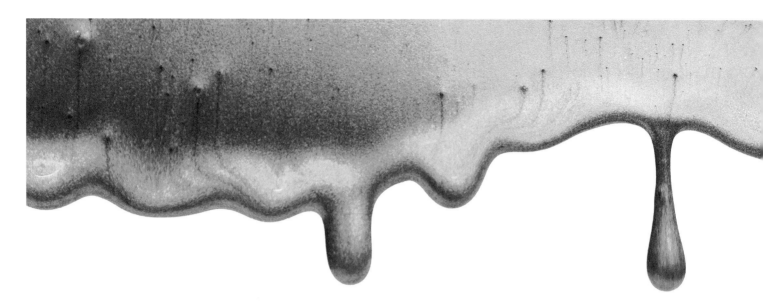

I CAN
&
I WILL
in Shaa Allaah

Spiritual Development

This category is all about nourishment of the SOUL

It's the first category of this journal because you can't be fully productive as a Muslim if your roots don't belong to Allah. If you keep growing branches around a root that's not strong enough on its own, the growth of the branches will eventually make the whole tree fall! As a tree, you have 5 roots which keep you standing!

1) Tawheed
This section contains exercises like understanding attributes of Allah through memorization of His 99 names and studying Qur'an (word of Allah) cover to cover.

2) Salah
This section contains one month charts to track your prayers and masnoon morning/evening adhkaar (remembrance of Allah).

3) Sawm
Fasting plan is to encourage you to have a personal commitment with yourself on how you can fast beyond Ramadan and complete your missed fasts (if any).

4) Zakat/Charity
Obligatory alms are yearly but the charity chart helps you embody the idea of giving every day, every week or every month (however much you are able to do).

5) Hajj
Hajj budget plan is to help you step closer to a reality of embarking on a journey of a lifetime through practical steps towards your dream!

Let's submit & grow these roots deeper into the soil because this tree has been created with a purpose. Let's not waste this precious gift from Our Creator.

Say, "Indeed,
my prayer,
my rites of sacrifice,
my living
and my dying
are for Allah,
Lord of the worlds.

[6:162]

قُلْ إِنَّ
صَلَاتِي
وَنُسُكِي
وَمَحْيَايَ
وَمَمَاتِي
لِلّٰهِ
رَبِّ الْعَالَمِينَ

I will
in Shaa Allaah

memorize 99 names of Allah

Memorization Tracker

#	Names of Allah	✔	#	Names of Allah	✔	#	Names of Allah	✔
1	Allaah الله		34	As-Salaam السَّلام (The Flawless One)		67	Al-Musawwir المُصَوِّر (The Bestower of Forms)	
2	Al-Ahad الأَحَد (The One/Unique)		35	As-Samee' السَّميع (The All Hearing)		68	Al-Muqtadir المُقْتَدر (The Omnipotent)	
3	Al-A'laa الأَعْلَى (The Most Exalted)		36	Ash-Shaakir الشَّاكِر (The Grateful)		69	Al-Muqeet المُقيت (The All Powerful Maintainer)	
4	Al-Akram الأَكْرَم (The Most Generous)		37	Ash-Shakoor الشَّكور (The Appreciative)		70	Al-Malik المَلك (The King)	
5	Al-Ilaah الإله (The One Who Alone Deserves to be Worshipped)		38	Ash-Shaheed الشَّهيد (The Witness)		71	Al-Maleek المَلِك (The Supreme Sovereign)	
6	Al-Awwal الأوَّل (The First)		39	As-Samad الصَّمَد (The Perfect Lord and Master Upon Whom All of the Creation Depends)		72	Al-Mawlaa المَوْلَى (The Master)	
7	Al-Aakhir الآخِر (The Last)		40	Al-'Aalim العَالِم (The All Knower)		73	Al-Muhaymin المُهَيْمِن (The Dominant One)	
8	Az-Zaahir الظاهِر (The Most High)		41	Al-'Azeez العَزيز (The Almighty)		74	An-Naseer النَّصِير (The Helper)	
9	Al-Baatin البَاطِن (The Most Near)		42	Al-'Azeem العَظيم (The Great)		75	Al-Waahid الوَاحِد (The One &Only)	
10	Al-Baari البَارِئ (The Originator)		43	Al-'Afuww العَفُوّ (The One Who Pardons Again&Again)		76	Al-Waarith الوَارِث (The Inheritor)	
11	Al-Barr البَرّ (The Most Kind)		44	Al-'Aleem العَليم (The All Knowing)		77	Al-Waasi' الوَاسِع (The Vast One)	
12	Al-Baseer البَصِير (The All Seeing)		45	Al-'Aliyy العَلِيّ (The Sublime)		78	Al-Wadood الوَدُود (The Loving)	
13	At-Tawwaab التَّوَّاب (The One Who Accepts the repentance)		46	Al-Ghaffaar الغَفَّار (The Oft-Forgiving)		79	Al-Wakeel الوَكِيل (The Trustee)	
14	Al-Jabbaar الجَبَّار (The Compeller)		47	Al-Ghafoor الغَفُور (The One Who Forgives Extensively)		80	Al-Waliyy الوَلِيّ (The Guardian)	
15	Al-Haafiz الحافِظ (The Protector)		48	Al-Ghaniyy الغَنِيّ (The Self Sufficient)		81	Al-Wahhaab الوَهَّاب (The Bestower)	
16	Al-Haseeb الحَسِب (The Sufficient)		49	Al-Fattaah الفَتَّاح (The Opener)		82	Al-Jameel الجَمِيل (The Beautiful)	
17	Al-Hafeez الحَفِيظ (The Preserver)		50	Al-Qaadir القَادِر (The Fully Able One)		83	Al-Jawaad الجَوَاد (The Munificent)	
18	Al-Hafee الحَفِيّ (The Benevolent)		51	Al-Qaahir القَاهِر (The Subduer)		84	Al-Hakam الحَكَم (The Judge)	
19	Al-Haqq الحَقّ (The Truth)		52	Al-Quddoos القُدُّوس (The Pure &Perfect)		85	Al-Hayyiyy الحَيِّ (The Modest)	
20	Al-Mubeen المُبِين (The Evident)		53	Al-Qadeer القَدِير (The All Powerful)		86	Ar-Rabb الرَّبّ (The Lord and Nurturer)	
21	Al-Hakeem الحَكِيم (The All-Wise)		54	Al-Qareeb القَرِيب (The Ever Near)		87	Ar-Rafeeq الرَّفِيق (The Gentle)	
22	Al-Haleem الحَلِيم (The Forbearing)		55	Al-Qawiyy القَوِيّ (The Strong)		88	As-Subbooh السُّبُّوح (The Perfect)	
23	Al-Hameed الحَمِيد (The Praiseworthy)		56	Al-Qahhaar القَهَّار (The Subjugator)		89	As-Sayyid السَّيِّد (The Lord & Master)	
24	Al-Hayy الحَيّ (The Ever Living)		57	Al-Kabeer الكَبِير (The Magnificent)		90	Ash-Shaafee الشَّافِي (The Healer)	
25	Al-Qayyoom القَيُّوم (The Self Sustaining)		58	Al-Kareem الكَرِيم (The Most Noble & Generous)		91	At-Tayyib الطَّيِّب (The Pure One)	
26	Al-Khabeer الخَبِير (The Fully Aware)		59	Al-Lateef اللَّطِيف (The Subtle &Kind)		92	Al-Qaabid القابِض (The Withholder)	
27	Al-Khaaliq الخَالِق (The Creator of Everything)		60	Al-Mu'min المؤمن (The Trustworthy Granter of Security)		93	Al-Baasit البَاسِط (The Expander)	
28	Al-Khallaaq الخَلَّاق (The Creator Who Creates Again & Again)		61	Al-Muta'aalee المُتَعَالِي (The Supreme)		94	Al-Muqaddim المُقَدِّم (The One Who Gives Precedence)	
29	Ar-Ra'oof الرَّؤُوف (The Compassionate)		62	Al-Mutakabbir المُتَكَبِّر (The Justly &Rightfully Proud)		95	Al-Mu'akhkhir المُؤَخِّر (The Delayer)	
30	Ar-Rahmaan الرَّحْمَان (The Extremely Merciful)		63	Al-Mateen المَتِين (The Firm One)		96	Al-Muhsin المُحْسِن (The Benevolent)	
31	Ar-Raheem الرَّحِيم (The Bestower of Mercy)		64	Al-Mujeeb المُجِيب (The Responsive)		97	Al-Mu'tee المُعْطِي (The Giver)	
32	Ar-Razzaaq الرَّزَّاق (The Great Provider)		65	Al-Majeed المَجِيد (The Glorious)		98	Al-Mannaan المَنَّان (The Benefactor)	
33	Ar-Raqeeb الرَّقِيب (The Watchful)		66	Al-Muheet المُحِيط (The All Encompassing)		99	Al-Witr الوتر (The One)	

"Allah has 99 Names, i.e., 100 minus 1, & whoever believes in their meanings & acts accordingly, will enter Paradise; & Allah is witr (1) & loves 'the witr' (i.e., odd numbers)." (Bukhari)

I will
in Shaa Allaah

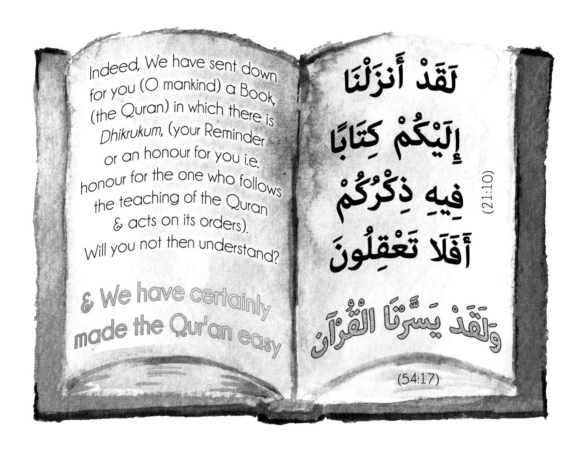

Indeed, We have sent down for you (O mankind) a Book, (the Quran) in which there is *Dhikrukum,* (your Reminder or an honour for you i.e. honour for the one who follows the teaching of the Quran & acts on its orders). Will you not then understand?

لَقَدْ أَنزَلْنَا إِلَيْكُمْ كِتَابًا فِيهِ ذِكْرُكُمْ أَفَلَا تَعْقِلُونَ

(21:10)

& We have certainly made the Qur'an easy

وَلَقَدْ يَسَّرْنَا الْقُرْآنَ

(54:17)

understand the whole Qur'an

Qur'an Log

#	JUZ' / PARA	Done	#	JUZ' / PARA	Done
01	الم (Al Fatiha 1 – Al Baqarah 141)		16	قَالَ أَلَم (Al Kahf 75 – Ta Ha 135)	
02	سَيَقُولُ (Al Baqarah 142 – Al Baqarah 252)		17	اقْتَرَبَ (Al Anbiyaa 1 – Al Hajj 78)	
03	تِلْكَ الرُّسُلُ (Al Baqarah 253 – Al Imran 92)		18	قَدْ أَفْلَحَ (Al Muminun 1 – Al Furqan 20)	
04	لَنْ تَنَالُوا (Al Imran 93 – An Nisaa 23)		19	وَقَالَ الَّذِينَ (Al Furqan 21 – An Naml 55)	
05	وَالْمُحْصَنَاتُ (An Nisaa 24 – An Nisaa 147)		20	أَمَّنْ خَلَقَ (An Naml 56 – Al Ankabut 45)	
06	لَا يُحِبُّ اللَّهُ (An Nisaa 148 – Al Ma'idah 81)		21	اتْلُ مَا أُوحِيَ (Al Ankabut 46 – Al Ahzab 30)	
07	وَإِذَا سَمِعُوا (Al Ma'idah 82 – Al An'am 110)		22	وَمَنْ يَقْنُتْ (Al Ahzab 31 – Ya Sin 27)	
08	وَلَوْ أَنَّنَا (Al An'am 111 – Al A'raf 87)		23	وَمَا لِيَ (Ya Sin 28 – Az Zumar 31)	
09	قَالَ الْمَلَأُ (Al A'raf 88 – Al Anfal 40)		24	فَمَنْ أَظْلَمُ (Az Zumar 32 – Fussilat 46)	
10	وَاعْلَمُوا (Al Anfal 41 – At Tauba 92)		25	إِلَيْهِ يُرَدُّ (Fussilat 47 – Al Jathiya 37)	
11	يَعْتَذِرُونَ (At Tauba 93 – Hud 5)		26	حم (Al Ahqaf 1 – Az Zariyat 30)	
12	وَمَا مِنْ دَابَّةٍ (Hud 6 – Yusuf 52)		27	قَالَ فَمَا خَطْبُكُمْ (Az Zariyat 31 – Al Hadid 29)	
13	وَمَا أُبَرِّئُ (Yusuf 53 – Ibrahim 52)		28	قَدْ سَمِعَ اللَّهُ (Al Mujadila 1 – At Tahrim 12)	
14	رُبَمَا (Al Hijr 1 – An Nahl 128)		29	تَبَارَكَ الَّذِي (Al Mulk 1 – Al Mursalat 50)	
15	سُبْحَانَ الَّذِي (Al Israa 1 – Al Kahf 74)		30	عَمَّ يَتَسَاءَلُونَ (An Nabaa 1 – An Nas 6)	

"...And none receive admonition except men of understanding...."
(3:7)

I will
in shaa Allaah

pray 5 times a day at prescribed times

Prayer Tracker

1) <u>Prayed at prescribed time</u> = color the first box green   ▮ Look at your progress by the end of a month.

2) <u>Prayed Late</u> (within its time limit) = color the second box red   ▮ If reds & blacks are more than greens, then repeat

3) <u>Didn't pray</u> (within its time limit) = color the third box black   ▮ till greens are most prominent in shaa Allaah.

PRAYERS	1	2	3	4	5	6	7	8	9	10	11	12	13	14	15	16	17	18	19	20	21	22	23	24	25	26	27	28	29	30	31
FAJR																															
ZUHR																															
ASR																															
MAGHRIB																															
ISHA																															

"Ibn Mas'ud said: "I asked the Messenger of Allah: 'O Messenger of Allah! Which is the most virtuous of deeds?' He said: 'Salat during its appropriate time.'" (Tirmidhi)

I will
in shaa Allaah

@artwithfaith

protect myself through adhkaar

Adhkaar Chart

DAYS	MORNING ADHKAAR	EVENING ADHKAAR
1		
2		
3		
4		
5		
6		
7		
8		
9		
10		
11		
12		
13		
14		
15		
16		
17		
18		
19		
20		
21		
22		
23		
24		
25		
26		
27		
28		
29		
30		

"& remember your Lord within yourself in humility & in fear without being apparent in speech - in the mornings & the evenings. & do not be among the heedless." (7:205)

I will
in shaa Allaah

fast beyond Ramadan

Fasting Plan

How can I introduce more fasting in my life:

WEEKLY	
MONTHLY	
YEARLY	

(number) _____ missed fasts to make up by _____ (time period)

(if you have a lot of missed fasts to make up, use this plan to complete them first)

In Paradise there is a gate called Rayyan. On the Day of Resurrection the call will go out; Where are those who used to fast? Whoever is among those will enter it & whoever enters it will never feel thirst again. **(Ibn Majah)**

I will
in shaa Allaah

give charity from what I love

Charity Chart

Different ways I can do charity & create sadaqah jaariyah for myself (in shaa Allaah)
[through words, money, actions, material goods, time etc.]

DAILY	
WEEKLY	
MONTHLY	
YEARLY	

"Never will you attain the good [reward] until you spend [in the way of Allah] from that which you love. & whatever you spend - indeed, Allah is Knowing of it.'" (3:92)

I will
in shaa Allaah

save money to go to Hajj

Hajj Budget Plan

Amount of money required to perform Hajj	
Savings I already have (that I can use for Hajj)	
Debts that need to be paid (if any)	
How much can I save per month to reach my goal?	
How much time will it take me to reach my goal?	

Different ways I can save money each month:

"...And [due] to Allah from the people is a pilgrimage to the House..." (03:97)

Short Term Goals

Long Term Goals

Highlight Your Productivity Score:

0 1 2 3 4 5
6 7 8 9 10

Notes

_"So when you have finished [your duties],
then stand up [for worship]." (94:7)_

Notes

"Verily, in the remembrance of Allah
do hearts find rest." (13:28)

Personal Development

This category is all about nourishment of the BODY

It covers the aspects of your body that are crucial to your productivity - starting from the energy inside of you to the vibes around you!

1) Self Love
This sections contains positive affirmations to build a sense of self worth and respect which leads to self confidence that's productive and not narcissistic.

2) Self Care
This is all about taking care of your body & mind. From daily/weekly/monthly self care goals for a quieter mind & calmer you to lifestyle goals for a healthy body inside out.

3) Self Awareness
Have you ever shed a tear without knowing what's wrong? Or felt constantly frustrated without any reason? Usually, we are so out of tune with our emotions that we are unable to point out what is it that's making us feel the way we feel! Hence awareness of yourself is crucial. This is why this section includes exercises like determining your strengths and weakness, good and bad habits etc.

4) Self Management
The next step of self evaluation is dealing with whatever you've found out about yourself in a way that makes you grow. Be it managing stress by tracking your mood or attaining clarity and focus through decluttering the space around and within, to make room for more reflection and productive work.

Let's beat your own record
& become better than you were yesterday!
Let's compare yourself with none but YOU!

Indeed, Allah

will not change

the condition of a people

until they change

what is in themselves.

إِنَّ اللَّهَ

لاَ يُغَيِّرُ

مَا بِقَوْمٍ

حَتَّى يُغَيِّرُواْ

مَا بِأَنْفُسِهِمْ

[13:11]

I will
in shaa Allaah

fill my jug before I fill other cups

Self-Care Goals

DAILY	WEEKLY	MONTHLY

"...your self has a right on you..." (Abi Dawud)

I will
in shaa Allaah

love myself the way Allah made me

Positive Affirmations

Things I love about myself alhamdulillah	Things others love about me alhamdulillah

"We have certainly created man in the best of stature" (95:4)

I will
in shaa Allaah

turn my weaknesses into my strengths

Self Exploration

My Weaknesses	My Strengths
How can I overcome them?	**How can I utilise them?**

"A strong believer is better and dearer to Allah than a weak one, and both are good..." (Muslim)

I will
in shaa Allaah

make healthy choices in my life

Health Goals

DAILY	WEEKLY	MONTHLY

"...There is nothing wrong with being rich for one who has piety, but good health for one who has piety is better than riches..." (Ibn Majah)

I will
in shaa Allaah

declutter my life to achieve better focus

Declutter Plan

Physical Decluttering What areas can I declutter/organise?	Mental Decluttering How can I lighten my mental load?

"Richness does not lie in the abundance of (worldly) goods but richness is the richness of the soul (heart, self)" (Muslim)

I will
in Shaa Allaah

bloom where I am planted

Self Awareness

Bad habits I want to break (things I want to do less of)	Good habits I want to cultivate (things I want to do more of)

"Look at those who are beneath you & don't look at those who're above you, for it's more suitable that you shouldn't consider as less the blessings of Allah."" (Ibn Majah)

I will
in shaa Allaah

take care of my mental health as much as my physical health

Stress Management

DAYS	Today I felt:	Because:
1		
2		
3		
4		
5		
6		
7		
8		
9		
10		
11		
12		
13		
14		
15		
16		
17		
18		
19		
20		
21		
22		
23		
24		
25		
26		
27		
28		
29		
30		

"No fatigue, nor disease, nor sorrow, nor sadness, nor hurt, nor distress befalls a Muslim, even if it were the prick he receives from a thorn, but that Allah expiates some of his sins for that." (Bukhari)

Short Term Goals	Long Term Goals

Highlight Your Productivity Score:

0 1 2 3 4 5
6 7 8 9 10

Notes

Messenger of Allah (ﷺ) said: "O Allah, bless my nation in their early mornings (i.e., what they do early in the morning)." (Ibn Majah)

Notes

The Prophet (ﷺ) said, "There are two blessings which many people lose: (They are) Health & free time (for doing good)." (Bukhari)

Strengthening Relationships

This category is all about nourishment of the HEART

Allah has brought you into this world where His other creations live and the relationship you have with them can highly affect your level of productivity.

Just like everything in life, you won't have perfection in terms of bonds and ties either. Which is why this section helps you make the most of them!

1) Relationship with Role Models from the Past

Our deen revolves around the teachings of our final Messenger of Allah
(Muhammad ﷺ)
Hence love for him (after Allah) = love for Islam. Which is why this sections hosts a Sunnah Habit Tracker because love doesn't merely reside in the heart, it outshines when it's strong enough! So get to know your role model better and choose his sunnahs that you can make a constant part of your life in shaa Allah.

2) Relationship with Family and Relatives

This section contains exercises to enhance your blood ties. Make your family a priority with effective time management and expressing love verbally and physically while maintaining ties with family of your family!

3) Relationship with Friends and Strangers

This section hosts exercises like social life tracker (to encourage you to befriend and connect to like minded people while subtracting the toxic people from your life (online or offline)), dawah plan (to spread the khair even among the strangers), giving and forgiving (to help you even turn enemies into friends).

Let's hope to stand beneath Allah's shade on the day of resurrection by loving others for His sake alone!

...& to parents do good

and to relatives,

orphans, & the needy.

And speak to people

good [words]...

وَبِالْوَالِدَيْنِ إِحْسَاناً
وَّذِي الْقُرْبَى
وَالْيَتَامَى وَالْمَسَاكِينِ
وَقُولُواْ لِلنَّاسِ
حُسْناً

[2:83]

I will
in Shaa Allaah

grow my love for Muhammad (P.B.U.H)

Sunnah Log

What are the ways I can grow my love for Rasool Allah (ﷺ)?

Through seeking of knowledge	Through application of knowledge

"Say (O Muhammad SAW to mankind): "If you (really) love Allah then follow me, Allah will love you..." (3:31)

I will
in shaa Allaah

prioritize my family over everything else

Life Priorities

Who are the people that matter the most in my life?	List of distractions that take my time away from them?	Steps I can take to balance my time better:

"Indeed each of you is a shepherd and all of you will be questioned regarding your flock..." (Tirmidhi)

I will
in shaa Allaah

express more love to my loved ones

Relationship Goals

Relationships I'd like to work on	Different ways I can work on them

"When one of you loves his brother,
then he should inform him of it." (Tirmidhi)

I will
in shaa Allaah

uphold the ties of kinship

Maintaining Kinship Ties

List of closest relatives I should stay in touch with	Ways to build a good relationship with them
List of distant relatives I can stay in touch with (descending order)	

"Anyone who wants to have his provision expanded & his term of life prolonged should maintain ties of kinship." (Al-Adab Al-Mufrad 56)

I will
in shaa Allaah

الْمَرْءُ مَعَ مَنْ أَحَبَّ

make friends who make me a better Muslim

Social Life Tracker

Positive influences in my life	Negative influences in my life
Ways to stay in touch with old friends & make new friends who boost my spirituality	Ways to manage toxic people who drain my spirituality

Anas b. Malik said: I never saw the Companions of Prophet ﷺ so happy about anything as I saw them happy about this thing. A man said : Messenger of Allah! A man loves another man for the good work which he does, but he himself cannot do like it. Prophet ﷺ said: A man will be with those whom he loves." (Abi Dawud)

I will
in shaa Allaah

forgive without a grudge & give without expectation

Personal Resolutions

Grudges that I have	Expectations that I have
How can I let them go?	**How can I give without expecting back?**

"Don't nurse malice against one another, don't nurse aversion against one another and don't be inquisitive about one another ..." (Muslim)

I will
in shaa Allaah

invite others to the beautiful deen of Allah

Dawah Plan

DAWAH MODES	How can I help a non-Muslim find Allah?	How can I help a non-practicing Muslim get closer to Allah?
OFFLINE		
ONLINE		

The Prophet (ﷺ) said: "Convey (my teachings) to the people even if it were a single sentence (an ayah)..." (Bukhari)

Short Term Goals | Long Term Goals

Highlight Your Productivity Score:

0 1 2 3 4 5
6 7 8 9 10

Notes

The Prophet (ﷺ) said: Those who do not show mercy to our young ones and do not realise the right of our elders are not from us. (Abi Dawud)

Notes

"Whosoever begins the day feeling family security & good health; & possessing provision for his day is as though he possesed the whole world." **(Tirmidhi)**

Goals
&
Dreams

This category is all about nourishment of the MIND

It's about having the drive to achieve & progressing towards your dreams to turn them into a reality through:

1) Vision (relying upon Allah)
This section revolves around discovering your dream and having a growth mindset; from dispelling self limiting behaviour and self doubts to shifting your perspective on failure and hardships...& most importantly, relying upon Allah.

2) Action (tying your camel)
This sections revolves around practical steps you can take to turn your vision into a reality in shaa Allaah. First of all, asking Allah for guidance and making dua with full conviction - even if it takes long, even if it seems impossible, pray for BIG goals! You don't have to settle for less with Allah.

Allah's Messenger (ﷺ) said: "when you ask Allah, ask Him for Al-Firdaus*."
[Tirmidhi]

*(In Paradise, there are a 100 levels, what is between every two levels is like what is between the heavens and the earth. Al-Firdaus is ts highest level, and from it the 4 rivers of Paradise are made to flow forth)

Secondly, gaining knowledge and learning skills required to achieve your goals and dreams. Take small measurable steps slowly but steadily to make your dreams believable and achievable. Each step matters. Achieve better productivity and joy at your own pace. Be the turtle that wins the race.

So let's decide!
One day or day one ?

And never say of anything,

"Indeed, I will do that tomorrow,"

Except [when adding],

"If Allah wills"

And remember your Lord

when you forget [it]

and say, "Perhaps my Lord

will guide me to what is nearer

than this to right conduct."

وَلاَ تَقُولَنَّ لِشَيْءٍ

إِنِّي فَاعِلٌ ذَلِكَ غَدًا

إِلاَّ

أَن يَشَاءَ اللَّه

ُ وَاذْكُر رَّبَّكَ

إِذَا نَسِيتَ

وَقُلْ عَسَى أَن

يَهْدِيَنِ رَبِّي لِأَقْرَبَ

مِنْ هَذَا رَشَدًا

[18:23-24]

71

I will
in Shaa Allaah

Offer 2 rak`at & say:

اللَّهُمَّ إِنِّي أَسْتَخِيرُكَ بِعِلْمِكَ وَأَسْتَقْدِرُكَ بِقُدْرَتِكَ،
وَأَسْأَلُكَ مِنْ فَضْلِكَ الْعَظِيمِ، فَإِنَّكَ تَقْدِرُ وَلاَ أَقْدِرُ
وَتَعْلَمُ وَلاَ أَعْلَمُ وَأَنْتَ عَلَّامُ الْغُيُوبِ،
اللَّهُمَّ إِنْ كُنْتَ تَعْلَمُ أَنَّ هَذَا الْأَمْرَ خَيْرٌ لِي فِي
دِينِي وَمَعَاشِي وَعَاقِبَةِ أَمْرِي فَاقْدُرْهُ لِي وَيَسِّرْهُ لِي
ثُمَّ بَارِكْ لِي فِيهِ، وَإِنْ كُنْتَ تَعْلَمُ أَنَّ هَذَا الْأَمْرَ
شَرٌّ لِي فِي دِينِي وَمَعَاشِي وَعَاقِبَةِ أَمْرِي فَاصْرِفْهُ
عَنِّي وَاصْرِفْنِي عَنْهُ، وَاقْدُرْ لِي الْخَيْرَ حَيْثُ كَانَ
ثُمَّ أَرْضِنِي بِهِ   (Istikhara Dua)

use the power of dua to fulfill my dreams

Dua Diary

What dreams would I achieve if I had few years to live?	Duas I can make for those dreams day in and day out	Important steps to do Istikhara for (to achieve my dreams)

"The Prophet (ﷺ) used to teach us the way of doing Istikhara (asking Allah to guide one to the right action concerning any job or a deed),in all matters as he taught us the Suras of the Qur'an..." (Bukhari)

I will
in shaa Allaah

To-Do List

✓ memorize Quran
✓ learn archery
  sacrifice an animal myself

check everything off my bucket list

Bucket List

Dreams to Fulfill	✓	Experiences to Undergo	✓

"If somebody intends to do a good deed &he doesn't do it,then Allah will write for him a full good deed;&if he intends to do a good deed &actually did it. then Allah will write for him (in his account) with Him (its reward) from 10 to 700 times to many more times..." (Bukhari)

I will
in Shaa Allaah

learn and teach a new skill

Skill Development

Skills I can teach others (online or offline)	Skills I can learn (based on my interests)

"When a person dies, his deeds are cut off except for three: Continuing charity, knowledge that others benefited from, & a righteous child who supplicates for him." (Tirmidhi)

I will
in shaa Allaah

رَبِّ زِدْنِي عِلْمًا

(20:114)

read more books

Book Log

Amazing books I have read	Amazing books I want to read

"Read! In the name of your Lord, Who has created (all that exists)" (96:1)

I will
in shaa Allaah

حَسْبُنَا اللّهُ وَنِعْمَ الْوَكِيلُ

take more risks through tawakkal Allah

Facing Fears

Risks I want to take	Fears that stop me from taking those risks	Steps I can take to prove that my trust in Allah is bigger than my fears

"A man said, "O Messenger of Allah, should I tie my camel & trust in Allah, or should I leave her untied & trust in Allah?" The Messenger of Allah ﷺ said, "Tie her & trust in Allah." (Tirmidhi)

I will
in shaa Allaah

see my failures as my ladder to success

Perspective Shift

Regrets from the past I want to let go of	Worries of the future I don't want to carry	Steps I can take to move forward

"None of you should say: 'My soul has become evil.' He should say: 'My soul is in bad shape.'" (Bukhari)

I will
in shaa Allaah

الْحَمْدُ لِلَّه
عَلَى كُلِّ
حَالٍ

grow through what I go through

Gratitude List

Hardships through which I grew	Positive lessons I learnt from them (Fill in the blank "Alhamdulillah for ____")

#AlhamdulillahForSeries

"How wonderful is the case of a believer: there's good for him in everything &this applies only to a believer. If prosperity attends him, he expresses gratitude to Allah &that's good for him: &if adversity befalls him, he endures it patiently &that is better for him". (Muslim)

Short Term Goals	Long Term Goals

Highlight Your Productivity Score:

0 1 2 3 4 5
6 7 8 9 10

Notes

"Take on only as much as you can do of good deeds, for the best of deeds is that which is done consistently, even if it is little." **(Ibn Majah)**

"Allah has hated for you three things:
1. Vain talks. (useless talk) that you talk too much or about others.
2. Wasting of wealth (by extravagance) -
3. And asking too many questions (in disputed religious matters) or asking others for something (except in great need)." **(Bukhari)**

Notes

Messenger of Allah (ﷺ) said, "Allah the Exalted has said: '...the most beloved thing with which My slave comes nearer to Me is what I've enjoined upon him' and My slave keeps on coming closer to Me through performing Nawafil (doing extra deeds besides what is obligatory) till I love him..." **(Bukhari)**

I COULD

&

I DID

alhamdulillah

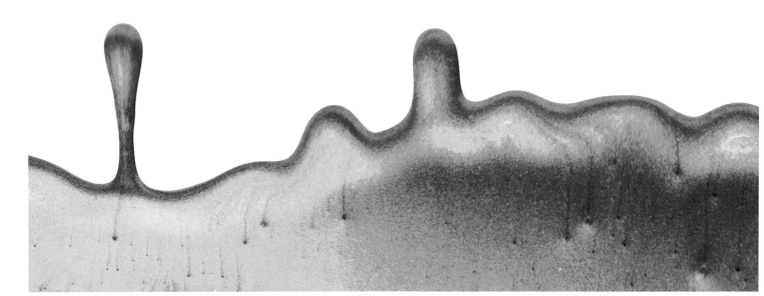

بَارَكَ اللهُ لَك
وجزاك اللهُ خيرًا

May Allāh bless you &
reward you [with]
goodness

'Abdullah bin 'Umar (May Allah be pleased with him) reported; Messenger of Allah (ﷺ) took hold of my shoulders and said,

كُنْ فِي الدُّنْيَا كَأَنَّكَ غَرِيبٌ أَوْ عَابِرُ سَبِيلٍ

"Be in the world like a stranger or a wayfarer."

Ibn 'Umar (May Allah be pleased with him) used to say: When you survive till the evening do not expect to live until the morning; and when you survive till the morning do not expect to live until the evening. While in good health (do good deeds) before you fall sick; and while you are alive (do good deeds) before death strikes.

[Bukhari]

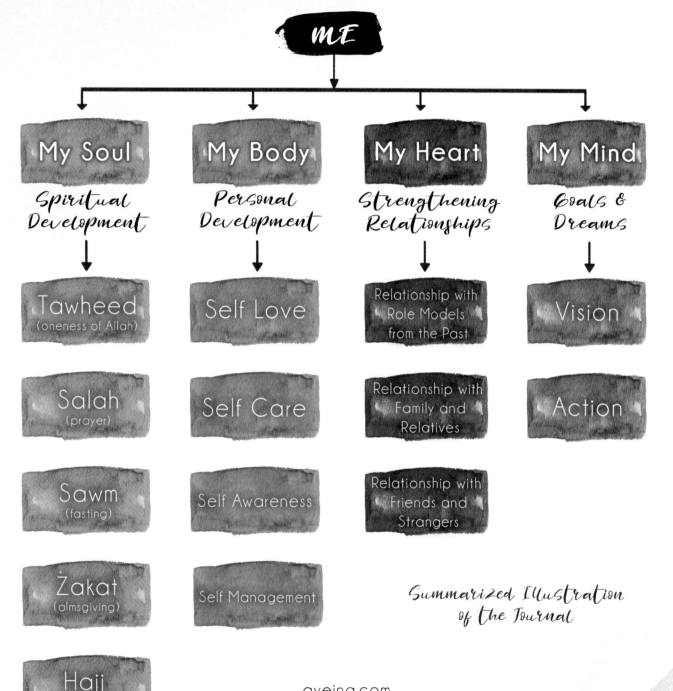

ME

My Soul	My Body	My Heart	My Mind
Spiritual Development	*Personal Development*	*Strengthening Relationships*	*Goals & Dreams*
Tawheed (oneness of Allah)	Self Love	Relationship with Role Models from the Past	Vision
Salah (prayer)	Self Care	Relationship with Family and Relatives	Action
Sawm (fasting)	Self Awareness	Relationship with Friends and Strangers	
Zakat (almsgiving)	Self Management		
Hajj (pilgrimage)			

Summarized Illustration of the Journal

ayeina.com

Submit your motivational captions or art for
#iWILLinshaAllah
by tagging us on:

@ayeina_official

 facebook.com/ayeina.online/

Subscribe to **ayeina.com** to receive
free extended printable bundles for:
Productivity Journal (2017) &
Gratitude Journal (2015)